Black History is All our History

A book celebrating 31 days of Black History Month

by Sally Penni MBE and illustrated by Julian D Penni

ISBN: 978-1-914933-10-3

Copyright 2021
All rights reserved. No part of this publication may be reproduced, stored in a retrieval system or transmitted in any form or by any means, electronic, mechanical, photocopy, recording or otherwise, without prior written consent of the copyright owner. Nor can it be circulated in any form of binding or cover other than that in which it is published and without similar condition including this condition being imposed on a subsequent purchaser.

The right of Sally Penni to be identified as the author of this work has been asserted in accordance with the Copyright Designs and Patents Act 1988.

A copy of this book is deposited with the British Library.

Published By:

i2i
PUBLISHING

i2i Publishing. Manchester.
www.i2ipublishing.co.uk

Dedication

To my three children for their love of learning.

Contents

Acknowledgements	7
About the Author	9
INTRODUCTION	11
WHAT IS BLACK HISTORY MONTH?	13
Paul Stephenson	21
Sarah Forbes Bonetta	25
John Kent	27
Lewis Hamilton	29
Diane Abbott	31
Olaudah Equiano	33
Sislin Fay Allen	35
John Anthony Roberts	37
Dame Linda Dobbs DBE	39
I. Stephanie Boyce	41
Kamala Harris	45
William Cuffay, 1788 – 1870	47
Mary Seacole, 1805-81	49
Samuel Coleridge-Taylor, 1875-1912	51
Claudia Jones, 1915-64	53
Olive Morris, 1952-79	55
Jack Leslie, 1901-88	57
Ottobah Cugoano	59
Walter Tull	61
Ena Collymore	63
The Windrush Generation	65
Cheddar Man	67
Eric Irons OBE	69
Sir Arthur Lewis	71
Paul Leroy Robeson	73
Some Role Models from Outside the UK	75
Nelson Mandela	77
Rosa Parks	79

Martin Luther King	81
Josephine Baker	83
Harriet Tubman	85
Challenges that remain today	87
Being an ally and being actively anti-racist	97
Being positive	101
Conclusion	103
Activities	105
Further Reading	107
Charities	109
Other books by Sally SJ Penni	111

Acknowledgements

First of all, it's hard work being a lawyer and a mother, so writing another book means there are people to thank. I have many people to thank for the support which has made it possible.

Second, there would not even be a book without my lovely children, who have been patient with my research and ideas for a book about black history. They are thrilled to have something to read in Black History Month and have conversation starters.

Third, my husband, who is patient with all of my projects and is forever asking why I am writing in the first place. Admittedly, this is said by him when I am writing legal documents! But he is astonished once he sees my books come to life covering important issues.

The illustrations in the book are by my brother Julian Penni, a talented artist, an architect by trade and a brilliant father of three. Even though he is very busy, he still found some time to draw the hidden figures from history.

Thank you, i2i Publishing.

During the completion of this book, the delayed Euro2020 football championship was played in 2021 during the Covid-19 pandemic. England made history by reaching the finals. However, due to three missed penalties from three black players, they received racist abuse through social media and Marcus Rashford's mural in Withington, Manchester, was defaced. The nation's response was to condemn such abuse and prove that love conquers racism, not hate. The incident proved that we still need to have conversations about race and racism in the UK and globally. I want to thank the people of Manchester for their support of me and my work, inside and outside the courtroom.

I also wish to extend my thanks to Marcus Rashford for all he does for child poverty. He was awarded his MBE in the same honours list as me, by her Majesty the Queen.

Finally, a massive, heartfelt thank you to you, my lovely readers. If you did not read my books, there would be no point in writing them for the children and, of course, all the grown-ups.

About the Author

Sally SJ Penni MBE

Sally SJ Penni MBE is a barrister at law and practices in Manchester and London. She is a Master of the Benches of Gray's Inn, a governor role, and one of the youngest black women to be so elected.

Sally was called to the bar in 2000 by the Honourable Society of Gray's Inn, London. She is the first barrister on the northern circuit, North-West of England, to be honoured in the Queen's birthday honours list, receiving an MBE in 2020. This honour was bestowed on her alongside footballer and food poverty campaigner Marcus Rashford, the Manchester United footballer, and Brian Cox, CBE, a former keyboard player with D:Ream and physicist.

Sally Penni specialises in Criminal Law and Employment Law, specialising in vulnerable witnesses and young offenders with protected characteristics. She is married with three children. She is an author and podcast host of Talking Law, with 60,000 listeners. Penni is the founder of Women in the Law UK.

INTRODUCTION

Each year in October we celebrate Black History Month. But who are these people, and who are the hidden figures we don't know about?

Most of us have heard of Nelson Mandela, Martin Luther King, Rosa Parks, and Malcolm X. Perhaps you have studied them in school when discussing discrimination?

In Britain, you may be familiar with sports stars such as Tessa Sanderson, Dame Kelly Holmes, boxer Nicola Adams, and Marcus Rashford, the footballer. But what about historical figures who were British?

In this book, we are going to celebrate the lesser-known figures that played a significant part in history, as well as some who are blazing a trail in the present. Prepare for a fantastically amazing journey as you meet Princess Sarah Bonetta, Paul Stephenson, Kamala Harris, Mary Seacole ... and many more!

The men and women in this book didn't set out to be thought of as great. They achieved extraordinary things simply by following their hearts, talents and dreams. They didn't listen when people said they couldn't do something. They dared to be different. *They made a difference.*

I hope at the end you will see black history is, in fact, all our history. From black Tudors and black soldiers to black princesses and professors in Britain.

Through a mix of 'Did You Know' sections and factual showcases, this book is written to dip in and out of. I hope you can see how black history fits into all aspects of the history we are taught at school. Whether in sport, in art, in politics, in discrimination and civil rights, black history is everywhere! I am not a historian, I am a practising lawyer. I do, however, love history and learning about where laws came from. I hope you enjoy learning about black history too.

Did you know?

There are laws that relate to black history in the UK. They are:

Abolition of Slavery Act (1833)
Race Relations Act (1965)
Sex Discrimination Acts (1975 and 1984)
Equality Act (2010)
Modern Slavery Act (2015)
Protection of Harassment Act (1997)

Racially aggravated offences are criminal offences. You will receive a worse sentence for your crime if it was based on someone's race.

WHAT IS BLACK HISTORY MONTH?

Black History Month, which is every October, is a chance to highlight the achievements and contributions of black people through the ages, as well as the struggles and barriers they still face in their daily lives.

Black History Month highlights historical episodes and figures not otherwise taught in UK schools. In this book, I would like to highlight just some of these. Black people have long been part of British history before Windrush and even slavery, from black Romans and Tudors to a black princess adopted by Queen Victoria and Prince Albert.

The following is a transcription of a video message given by Prime Minister Boris Johnson in October 2020. It summarises what we have always known – that black history is all our history. (You can view the full speech here: https://t.co/7jlrsAzwY1).

"For countless generations, people of African and Caribbean descent have been shaping our nation's story, making a huge difference to our national and cultural life and helping to make Britain a better place to be. It is this contribution of black British people that I am proud to be celebrating.

That contribution is overwhelmingly apparent today in the energy, talent and dedication of business leaders, lawyers, academics, musicians, artists, and many more. This year, we have seen the heroic efforts of all frontline workers and the doctors, nurses and medical professionals who have been tirelessly supporting our NHS throughout the coronavirus pandemic.

Of course, there is much more work to be done to ensure that every person of every skin colour, background and creed has the opportunity to succeed, and to stamp out discrimination and racism. I understand the force and depth of feeling that has been expressed following the death of George Floyd in the United States and share the determination of all those seeking a more equal and just world. That's why I have set up a Commission on Race and Ethnic Disparities to make the progress so many have called for, and to bring about lasting change.

But I also believe that alongside tackling the substance of the problem, we should be giving due praise and recognition to all those who have played such an important role in helping to positively shape modern Britain and our modern Commonwealth.

It's a great shame that more people do not know more about Paul Stephenson or Mary Prince. Or that they haven't heard about the many brave black servicemen who served in the World Wars – from those grappling in the mud of the Western Front, to the valiant Caribbean pilots and aircrew in the Second World War, and the heroes who fought further afield, in places such as Burma. Or even that they know so little about the Windrush generation, from the nurses who were there at the very start of our NHS to all those who helped rebuild our country after the war.

A key part of the commission's work will be to look at how we ensure society is more aware of the significant role people from different ethnic backgrounds have played in our shared British history. Let's use this Black History Month to celebrate not just the achievements of people today, but of all those who have shaped our nation. Let's raise up those names. Let's remember their acts. And let's celebrate them – because black British history is all our history."

However, with black people and minorities still being asked frequently, 'where are you from?', I wondered if it would be interesting to celebrate some of the everyday history we don't always learn at school.

Now, I cannot include all of them in this book, but I hope you will see from reading it that it features interesting people from all our history. I am not a historian, but I am a girly swot. My day job is a barrister at law. I appear in courts. I use old laws written largely by white men from previous centuries. Orchestras play music mainly written by white men.

But what about the black classicists that came before the Kanneh-Mason family who played at Prince Harry's wedding?

What about the slaves who built the theatres and statues in the UK?

Black History Overview

In all aspects of history, black people were present and made a contribution, from the music halls and concert halls built by slaves to the rebuilding of Britain and the creation of the NHS following World War II. Here is a brief overview of some significant events in black history:

Era	Length and Timeline	Significant Events
The Romans	27BC-AD476	Black Roman body discovered, which means there were black Romans in York.
		Roman Africans guarded Hadrian's Wall in the North-East of England.
Tudors	1485-1603	John Blanke, trumpet player, petitioned Henry VIII for an increase in wages.
Stuarts	1603-1714	

The early Georgians	1714-1776	Images of well-dressed black children in paintings.
The late Georgians	1777-1837	
The Victorians	1837-1901	Queen Victoria adopted a tenth child, Sarah Bonetta, a black African slave.
	1862-3	Mill workers in Rochdale protested against slaves being used in the cotton trade.
The 20th century		
The First World War – WWI	1914-1919	Black troops recruited to fight in the war. Soldiers from colonies, Gurkhas, black African and Indian troops all fought and died.
	1919	Liverpool race riots.
The Second World War – WWII	1939-1945	Black American soldiers fighting in the war.
Windrush	1948	HMS Windrush brings Caribbean people to the UK to help rebuild the UK after the war.

Here are 10 histories I did not know. Did you?

1. West Indian soldiers in World War I

15,204 men served in the British West Indies Regiment, from the Bahamas to British Guiana, however, they have largely been forgotten in Remembrance commemorations.

The soldiers faced racism from their comrades and enemies and weren't allowed to fight alongside white soldiers. Nevertheless, they carried out dangerous jobs such as loading ammunition, digging trenches, and laying telephone wires.

After moving to Italy following armistice, the soldiers mutinied, no longer willing to suffer the humiliation of cleaning clothes and latrines for white soldiers who themselves received pay rises. One soldier was executed, others imprisoned, and they were all excluded from the victory parades marking the end of the war.

2. The Bristol bus boycott

In 1963, after 18-year-old Guy Bailey was turned away from a job interview at the state-owned Bristol Omnibus Company because he was black (which was legal at the time), members of the black community, organised by Paul Stephenson, Roy Hackett and Bailey, led a boycott of the buses in protest. After four months, the bus company relented, overturning the ban on ethnic minorities working on Bristol's buses. This marked a significant step towards the UK's first laws against racial discrimination, resulting in the Race Relations Act 1965, now part of the Equality Act 2010.

3. The Notting Hill Carnival in London

Notting Hill carnival in London is the largest street party in Europe. It began when human rights activist Claudia Jones, herself deported from the US for being a member of the Communist party and granted asylum in the UK, threw herself into anti-racist activism.

In response to the Notting Hill riots of 1958 and the racist murder of Kelso Cochrane, Jones launched an indoor Caribbean carnival in St Pancras in 1959 with the intention of bringing people together. Further indoor events were held throughout the 1960s, finally taking to the streets of Notting Hill in 1965. Notting Hill Carnival is now second only in size to Brazil's Rio carnival.

4. John Blanke, the black trumpeter

The Tudor period was significant for black settlement in Britain, although seldom mentioned in schools. John Blanke, a regular musician at the courts of both King Henry VII and Henry VIII, was one such settler. He is the first known black Briton for whom we have both their name and picture. A 60ft-long scroll commissioned by Henry VIII depicting the extravagant Westminster Tournament of 1511 shows John riding on horseback in the royal procession.

John was paid 8d a day in wages. This doubled to 16d after he successfully petitioned the king for a pay rise.

5. 'Beachy Head woman'

A mysterious, ancient skeleton of the 'Beachy Head woman', believed to be the first known person in Britain from sub-Saharan Africa, was uncovered in a village in East Sussex. She is thought to have lived nearly 1,800 years ago in AD245, the middle of the Roman period in Britain.

6. 'Ivory bangle lady'

The 'ivory bangle lady', a middle-class woman of black African ancestry and one of the wealthiest inhabitants of fourth century Roman York, was discovered in 1901 inside a stone sarcophagus. She was surrounded by jewellery made of Yorkshire jet and African elephant ivory, a glass mirror and a blue glass jug. Her discovery challenged assumptions that Africans in Britain at the time were poor or slaves.

7. Britain's black miners

In the aftermath of the second world war, amid severe labour shortages in the mining industry, black workers were invited to Britain by the government to fill vacancies in vital industries, including coalmines.

Hundreds of African-Caribbean men are estimated to have worked in the mines in Nottinghamshire, Leicestershire, Yorkshire, Bristol, Kent, Durham, South Wales and Scotland. At least a quarter of the workforce at Gedling Colliery in Nottingham, known as 'The Pit of Nations', were black.

8. The sacking of Benin

Benin City was one of the oldest states in West Africa, dating back to the 11th century. In 1897, during the 'Benin expedition', British troops punitively sacked the ancient city after it imposed customs duties which defied the British Empire. The city's walls – four times the length of the Great Wall of China – were razed. The city was burned to the ground and its treasures were looted.

Many of Benin's stolen artworks and artefacts were taken to Britain, auctioned or gifted to museums across Europe. Hundreds of these artefacts still reside in museums across the UK. The Benin bronzes remain the subject of demands for repatriation.

9. The Haitian Revolution

The Haitian Revolution was one of the largest slave rebellions in history, ending slavery in France's most profitable colony. The slave population of Saint-Domingue in the 18th century outnumbered the white population by ten to one. In 1791, the enslaved began a rebellion against white landowners, led by Haitian-born Toussaint L'Ouverture, a former slave. Haiti became the first independent black republic in the Americas in 1804.

10. The British Black Panthers

In 1968, the BBP was founded by Obi Egbuna in Notting Hill, London, inspired by the American Black Power movement. Under Altheia Jones-LeCointe's leadership from 1970, it transformed into a highly effective organisation rooted in working-class solidarity and community activism. The Panthers focused on fighting racial discrimination in jobs, education, health, and housing.

During a protest against police brutality, nine black leaders (known as the Mangrove Nine), were arrested and charged with inciting a riot. After representing themselves and demanding an all-black jury, they were acquitted. Evidence of racial hatred in the London police was publicly acknowledged by the judge.

Did you know?

Up to 300 Africans lived in Britain in the Tudor period.

Ready to meet 31 black figures who have played a significant part in British history and are shaping our modern world? Let's begin…

Paul Stephenson

The moment in 1964 when Paul Stephenson sat down in a pub that banned black people was the moment he helped change Britain's discrimination laws.

When Paul walked into the Bay Horse pub in Bristol and ordered half a pint, the pub's manager told him to get out, saying: "We don't want you black people in here – you are a nuisance." Stephenson refused. He was arrested and detained in a police cell until midnight.

In 1964, banning black and Asian people from pubs and working men's clubs, and even housing and jobs, was legal in the UK. At the time that Stephenson performed his 'sit-in' at the pub in protest, he had already led a successful boycott of the city's bus company.

Following the pub sit-in, Stephenson was put on trial, which made national headlines. Eight officers, each with different versions of events, claimed that he was "aggressive" and had tried to "force his way back into the pub" which was later found to be untrue. Harold Wilson, Prime Minister at the time, sent Stephenson a personal telegram to say he would change the law. And so, in 1965, the first Race Relations Act was formed to outlaw discrimination.

Growing up

Paul Stephenson was born in Rochford, Essex, in 1937. Aged three, he was evacuated to a care home in Great Dunmow, Essex, with seven white children, living there for seven years. He spent his time playing in the fields and paddling in streams and made lifelong friends.

Stephenson felt like an outsider when he returned to London in 1947, with shouts of "blackie", "monkey" and the N-word on his walk to school. From 1948, when immigration from the colonies increased, so did the racism. While at secondary school, and being the only black child in his class, Stephenson was no longer cute and a 'curiosity' as in his childhood, but instead was seen as a racial threat. While being caned, a teacher asked him: "Why are you looking so black?"

Later years

Stephenson joined the RAF as a cadet in 1953 and served until 1960. After the RAF, he went to college to study youth work, then moved to Bristol to become a youth and community development worker and supply teacher. Then came the bus boycott.

As the spokesman for the protesters, Stephenson won an important legal battle. However, not everyone agreed with his stance. Bill Smith, of the city's West Indian Association, believed that the protest undermined racial harmony in the city, with the Bishop of Bristol also in agreement. Those who did stand on the side of equality paid a high price. Learie Constantine, a cricketing star turned Trinidad's high commissioner, was removed from his post by the Trinidadian prime minister for his involvement.

Stephenson's activism garnered international attention. In 1964 he was invited to the US by the National Association for the Advancement of Coloured People (NAACP). He travelled to New York City, where he met Louis Farrakhan (then Louis X), and then went on to Richmond, in the US's segregated south, where he was met with hostility at his all-white hotel. Unbeknown to Stephenson, the NAACP had secured an agreement to desegregate the hotel and he was their test case – the first black man to stay at the John Marshall Hotel.

In 1974, Stephenson met Muhammad Ali in a hotel lobby, addressing him as Ali when many people still called him Cassius Clay, and asked him to visit his Brixton school. Ali agreed. Ali and Stephenson became friends and set up the Muhammad Ali

Sports Development Association (MASDA) to give inner-city youth access to sport. In 1982, MASDA launched the British Standing Conference Against Apartheid Sports with the support of the World Boxing Association (WBA) champion Lloyd Honeyghan.

In 1992, Stephenson returned to Bristol with his wife. He fostered eight children and campaigned for the city to acknowledge its links with slavery. In 2008, Stephenson became the first black man to be made Freeman of the City. Because of Paul Stephenson, we now have laws that protect all people from discrimination.

Sarah Forbes Bonetta

The Black Princess

Queen Victoria and her husband Prince Albert had nine children. But did you know that they also adopted a tenth child?

In 1848, orphan Sarah Forbes Bonetta was captured by the merciless King of Dahomey. She was only five years old. Before she too could be killed, Sarah was rescued by British naval officer Frederick who persuaded Sarah's captors to present the child as a 'gift' to Victoria. Frederick and Sarah sailed back to England on his ship, HMS Bonetta, which became her adopted name.

Princess Sarah Forbes Bonetta grew up with Queen Victoria's children around her and was treated like a member of the queen's biological family. The young princess married wealthy businessman Captain James Davies in 1862 and died of tuberculosis in 1880 at the age of 37.

John Kent

Britain's First Black Policeman

John Kent was born in Cumbria in 1805, beginning his duties as a police officer in Maryport in 1835 before joining Carlisle Police in 1837. John was the son of Thomas Kent, a slave who was brought into Whitehaven and freed in the UK.

It was previously thought that the first black police officer joined the Metropolitan Police in the 1960s. However, research found that John Kent served as an officer more than 100 years earlier.

Norwell Lionel Roberts QPM was the first black police officer to join London's Metropolitan Police, rising to the rank of Detective Sergeant. He was awarded the Queen's Police Medal in 1996.

A blue plaque was unveiled to commemorate John. Ian Bulman, a descendent of John who works on a dairy farm in Carlisle, said he was "pleased and proud", adding that he had a "lot of admiration of what John and his father went through."

What are blue plaques?

Blue plaques commemorate the link between a location and an individual who was regarded as 'eminent' in their field.

Lewis Hamilton

Formula One Racing Driver

Sir Lewis Hamilton MBE was born in Stevenage in 1985. Aged five, Hamilton's dad bought him a radio-controlled car which began his fascination with racing. The following year, Hamilton was placed second against adults in the British Radio Car Association (BRCA). Aged six, his father bought him a go-kart for Christmas and promised to support his racing career as long as he worked hard at school.

Hamilton began karting in 1993 and quickly began winning races and cadet class championships. At the age of ten, he became the youngest driver to win the British cadet karting championship and was signed to the McLaren young driver programme in 1998.

Hamilton has since won seven world titles and has overtaken Michael Schumacher's record of 91 wins in Formula One.

Having experienced bullying and racism as a child, Lewis now uses his platform to raise awareness of issues in sport and aims to leave a legacy for a sport that lacks representation. He is a major contributor to Great Ormond Street hospital, Unicef, the Honeypot Children's Charity and Children of Africa. He has also set up the Lewis Hamilton Foundation to provide grants and donations to help with disabilities, education and training, the advancement of health, and prevention or relief of poverty.

Diane Abbott

First Black Woman MP in England

Did you know?

The first non-white Members of Parliament were elected in 1987 for the Labour Party.

Diane Abbott is a British politician who has been a Member of Parliament for Hackney North and Stoke Newington since 1987. Her school openly opposed to her applying to Cambridge University. Nevertheless, Diane Abbott fought racism – and her own party – to become Britain's first black female MP. She was called an 'extremist' by opponents and treated as a liability by Labour.

Despite having endured much criticism and abuse in recent years, Diane Abbott has been a true voice and advocate for change.

Olaudah Equiano

Abolitionist

Olaudah Equiano was born in 1745 in the Eboe province (southern Nigeria). At around the age of 11, he was kidnapped with his sister, sold by local slave traders, and shipped across the Atlantic to Barbados and then Virginia.

In Virginia he was sold to Lieutenant Michael Pascal, a Royal Navy officer, who renamed him Gustavus Vassa after the 16th-century Swedish king. For eight years, Equiano travelled the oceans with Pascal, during which time he was baptised and learned to read and write.

Equiano was sold to a ship captain in London who took him to Montserrat and resold him to Robert King, a prominent merchant. While working as a deckhand, valet and barber for King, Equiano earned money by trading on the side. Only three years later, he had enough money to buy his freedom.

For the next twenty years, Equiano travelled the world, visiting places including the Arctic and Turkey. In 1786, he became involved in the movement to abolish slavery and was a prominent member of the 'Sons of Africa', a group of 12 black men campaigning for abolition.

In 1789, Equiano published his autobiography, *The Interesting Narrative of the Life of Olaudah Equiano or Gustavus Vassa, the African,* one of the earliest books published by a black writer. The book became popular and helped the abolitionist cause. In 1792, Equiano married Susanna Cullen and they had two daughters. Equiano died in 1797, aged 52.

Sislin Fay Allen

Britain's First Black Policewoman

> Did you know?
>
> Norwell Lionel Roberts was the first black police officer to join London's Metropolitan police. He enlisted in 1967, rising to the rank of Detective Sergeant.

Sislin Fay Allen joined the Metropolitan Police in 1968, becoming the first black WPC.

Sislin Fay Allen saw an advert appealing for male and female police officers while flicking through a newspaper. At the time, there were no black female officers, so the mum-of-two sat down and wrote an application. Within a few weeks, Sislin had made it to the interview stage and was accepted into the force.

The first prejudices Sislin experienced came from her own community for joining the police force. The perception of the police was poor, and the role was considered degrading. After her training and passing out ceremony Sislin was stationed in Croydon so she could be close to her family. She later transferred to Scotland Yard and then Norbury police station.

Sislin's appointment as the Metropolitan Police's first black female police officer prompted some hate mail, which she was never shown.

In 1972, Sislin left the Metropolitan Police and returned to her husband's birth country of Jamaica with their children. She joined the Jamaican police force before later returning to the UK with her family and settling in South London.

John Anthony Roberts

First Black QC at Queen's Counsel

John Anthony Roberts was the first lawyer of African ancestry to be a QC at Queen's Counsel, the highest ranking for barristers. He was also the first black lawyer to be the head of his chambers, to be made a Recorder of the Crown Court, and to be appointed by the British government to a dependent territory as a High Court Judge of the Supreme Courts of the British Virgin Islands & Anguilla, British West Indies. John was also the first Head of Chambers to accept seven female barristers as tenants in 1975, a record during that era.

John worked as a civil servant in the UK between 1964 and 1969. In 1966, driven by the desire to help people, he started to read law part-time at the Inns of Court School of Law.

John was called to the bar (Gray's Inn) in 1969, becoming a Master in 1996, and helped set up a chambers at 9 Stone Buildings, Lincoln's Inn, in 1970. Later, in 1975, he set up his own chambers at 2 Stone Buildings, ensuring that his set of chambers was fully representative, mixed and diverse with Asian, white, black African and Caribbean members.

John took silk in 1988 and was the first person of African origin to do so and later became a High Court Judge in the British Virgin Islands & Anguilla, both British West Indies Dependent Territories.

John was called to the bars of 10 other countries: Jamaica (1973), Sierra Leone (1975), Trinidad & Tobago (1978), Bahamas (1984), St Kitts & Nevis (1988), Antigua (2002), Barbados (2002), Bermuda (2003), Anguilla (2006) and Grenada (2007).

John was known as a modest and humble man, continuing to serve following his retirement, as President of the British West Indian Ex-Servicemen and Ex-Service Women's Association, as well as serving as joint President of the British Caribbean Association.

Dame Linda Dobbs DBE

Britain's First Black Judge

Dame Linda Penelope Dobbs, DBE, a retired High Court judge in England and Wales, served from 2004 to 2013. Dobbs was the first non-white person to be appointed to the senior judiciary of England and Wales.

In 2004, following a successful career at the bar, Dame Linda became the first non-white high court judge in the UK. At the bar, she was a member of a number of committees, including the Race Relations, Equal Opportunities, International, Professional Conduct and Professional Standard Committees. She became the Chairman of the Criminal Bar Association in 2003, setting up its first Equality and Diversity sub-committee.

During her time on the High Court Bench, Dame Linda was the Chair of the Magisterial Committee of the Judicial Studies Board, Senior Liaison Judge for Diversity, and Chair of the International Committee of the Judicial College and a Fawcett Commissioner.

Dame Linda has been involved in the training of lawyers and judges both in the UK and internationally for over 20 years and is a contributor and editor to a number of legal publications. She and is the director of training at the Judicial Institute for Africa, based at the University of Cape Town, where she is an honorary professor. She is a patron of a number of charities (including two in Sierra Leone and two in South Africa) and sits on a number of advisory committees. She is the immediate past President of ILFA (International Lawyers for Africa) and chair of the UK-Sierra Leone Pro Bono Network. Dame Linda is a patron of the African Prisons Project and an initiator of the 18 Red Lion Court Award for African advocates. She is also patron of Masicorp, an NGO promoting education in Masiphumelele, South Africa.

Dame Linda has been named as one of Britain's most powerful black women and one of the 100 Great Black Britons, featuring regularly in the Power List 100 of Influential Black Britons.

> Did you know?
>
> Tunde Akewole is the youngest governor of the Inns of Court.

I. Stephanie Boyce

Did you know?

I. Stephanie Boyce will become the first black president of the Law Society of England and Wales in 2021. The Law Society is the professional body for all solicitors.

In October 2021, I. Stephanie Boyce will become the 177th president, the sixth female and the first non-white person to hold the post in the history of the Law Society of England and Wales.

I. Stephanie's story

"I began my life journey in Aylesbury, Buckinghamshire, a place where I would come back to time and time again. Aylesbury in the 1970s when I was growing up there was a small country, sleepy market town with little ethnic diversity compared to today's diverse large ancient market town.

I grew up with the sounds of injustices ringing in my ears. Domestically and globally, I could see people struggling to exercise their rights and this is what inspired me to join the legal profession. To become a solicitor.

After living in Aylesbury for a number of years, at the age of 12 I went to live in America with my mother. America would have a lasting impression upon me, I would be overwhelmed by the poverty, the injustices, people unable to access justice because of their low socio-economic position, people struggling to exercise their rights, people having little or no rights because of the colour of their skin, oh how I longed to make a difference to have my voice heard. To encourage and inspire the voiceless to speak.

In 1991, I returned to the UK to live and study, but not before I came across my first barrier. My US qualification, my high school diploma was not enough to allow me entry to a British university. I would spend another two years undertaking an access to higher qualification diploma. This enabled me to enter London Guildhall University as it was then named in February 1996 as a part time student, whilst working part-time at British Rail. By September of that year, I had enrolled full-time leaving behind my life in Aylesbury and all things familiar, packing up my worldly goods in my car and heading to Mile End, but how I longed for home, the familiarity of that ole market town, the parish church of St Mary, the canal, the views of the town and beyond.

In June 1999 I graduated with an LLB(Hons) with politics. In September 1999 I entered the College of Law, Guildford where I would study and complete the Legal Practice Course (LPC), the final academic qualification on my route to becoming a solicitor. In 2000, the year of the Millennium Bug, I commenced my training contract, the last hurdle to becoming a qualified solicitor. Again, I would return to Aylesbury, the 'spiritual cradle of the Paralympics', the place where my dream had started all those years ago as a young child with a dream. I would commence my training contract, my two-year training period in the historic part of Aylesbury, Temple Street, with a local firm, a stone's throw from Bucks County Museum in Church Street.

Having walked into the firm for the first time as a trainee solicitor in 2000, I would walk out for the final time as a qualified solicitor in 2002, an officer of the court, with an overriding duty to the rule of law and the administration of justice.

The legal profession in general, and solicitors specifically, have a clear role to play in championing the values and concepts of justice, fairness, equity, and legitimacy, and never more so than now. I'm often reminding myself to not lose my joy in the difficulties of life, to keep my joy through the difficulties. I write this in the middle of a pandemic called Coronavirus 19, which has claimed the lives worldwide of over 780,000 people, no country, no place has been left untouched. The virus is a stark reminder that life is precious and for living. Many dreams have been placed on hold whilst we wait for the virus to pass and a vaccine to be found. If but not for the pandemic I would now be the Vice President of the Law Society, instead I remain the deputy Vice President, a delay of three months to allow colleagues and I the opportunity to deal with the impact of the pandemic on the profession.

In October 2021 I will become the 177th, the sixth female and the first non-white person to hold the post in the history of the Law Society of England and Wales. I am determined to leave the legal profession more diverse and inclusive than the one I entered. That more must be done to remove barriers, open doors and confront unacceptable behaviours that do not allow everyone the opportunity to succeed and make the most of their talents regardless of their race, gender, disability, sexuality, religion or background.

My story is one of resilience and determination, a burning desire to stand by my dream until it was realised, a definite purpose and one I was prepared to stand by until it was achieved. 'Four times', it took me four times before I was successfully elected as deputy Vice President. I was not prepared to quit because of temporary setbacks.

If you have ever been discouraged, faced difficulties that have taken the very soul out of you, marooned you in the desert of despair, been knocked back, faced hurdles, that no matter where you are in life, you too can reach your full potential if you are willing to get into action. To train your mind towards your definite purpose. To never quit." (Bucks County Museum, 2020)

You can read the original article here: www.buckscountymuseum.org/museum/stephanies-story-black-history-month.

Kamala Harris

First Black Vice President of USA

Kamala Harris is not in the UK, but as I finished writing this book, Kamala Harris became the first black Vice President of the USA, to President Joe Biden.

Kamala's heritage is Indian and Jamaican. She was born in the USA. Prior to becoming Vice President of the USA, she was a lawyer and prosecutor. This change means a lot to women and black minorities everywhere, not just in the USA. The Biden and Harris presidency succeeded the Donald J Trump and Mike Pence presidency.

William Cuffay, 1788 – 1870

Chartist Leader in Early Victorian London

Born on a merchant ship in the West Indies in 1788, William Cuffay was the son of a naval cook and former enslaved person from St Kitts. The family eventually settled in Chatham, Kent.

Cuffay played a leading role in the Chartist movement and was elected to the national executive of the National Charter Association in 1842. In August 1848, Cuffay was arrested for conspiring to levy war against the Queen. He was sentenced to transportation to Tasmania.

Mary Seacole, 1805-81

The Black Florence Nightingale

Mary Seacole was born in Kingston, Jamaica, in 1805, to her Jamaican mother and Scottish father. Mary learnt her nursing skills from her mother who kept a boarding house for wounded soldiers. Despite being of mixed race, Mary and her family had few civil rights. They couldn't vote or enter many professions.

In 1854, after travelling to England, Mary approached the War Office, asking to be sent to the Crimea as a war nurse. The War

Office refused. Undeterred, Mary funded her own trip and established the British Hotel for sick and convalescent soldiers, often risking her life on the frontline to tend to the dying and wounded.

After the war, Mary returned to England and became destitute and unwell. After the press highlighted her plight, a benefit festival was organised in Kennington, south London, in July 1857 to raise money for her. The fundraiser is believed to have attracted thousands of people. Later than year, Seacole published her memoirs, *The Wonderful Adventures of Mrs Seacole in Many Lands*.

Mary Seacole died on 14 May 1881. A statue of Seacole was erected opposite the Houses of Parliament in the grounds of St Thomas' hospital in 2016.

Samuel Coleridge-Taylor, 1875-1912

Black Classical Composer

Samuel Coleridge-Taylor was born in Holborn, London, on 15 August 1875 and was raised in Croydon. He was one of few black classical composers to catch the imagination of the white British musical establishment, coming to prominence in 1898 at the Gloucester festival with an orchestral *Ballade in A Minor*, followed by his much-acclaimed trilogy, *Hiawatha's Wedding Feast* (1898).

Coleridge-Taylor died aged 37 after he collapsed at West Croydon station while waiting for a train. His funeral procession through Croydon was lined for three and a half miles by crowds with their heads bared.

Claudia Jones, 1915-64

Founder of the Notting Hill Carnival

Born in Belmont, Port-of-Spain, Trinidad, in 1915, Claudia Jones lived much of her life in New York before she was deported from the US for being an active member of the US Communist party. She was given asylum in England in 1955. In England, Claudia threw herself into anti-racist activism and is considered the founder of the Notting Hill Carnival.

In response to the Notting Hill riots of 1958 and the racist murder of Kelso Cochrane, Jones launched an indoor Caribbean carnival in St Pancras in 1959 with the intention of bringing people together. Further indoor events were held throughout the 1960s, finally taking to the streets of Notting Hill in 1965. Notting Hill Carnival is now second only in size to Brazil's Rio carnival.

Olive Morris, 1952-79

Youth Member of the Black Panther Movement

Born in Jamaica in 1952, Olive Morris moved to south London as a young child with her siblings to be with her parents.

Olive was just 17 when she became a leading figure in Britain's anti-racism movement in the 1960s and 70s. She took action against discrimination in housing and employment, attacks by far-right groups such as the National Front, and the stop and search of black people. Morris was a member of the youth section of the Black Panther movement in the UK.

Olive became ill while on holiday in Spain and was diagnosed with non-Hodgkin's lymphoma, a form of cancer, upon her return home. She died on 12 July 1979 aged 27 at St Thomas' hospital in London.

Jack Leslie, 1901-88

Footballer

Jack Leslie was a successful footballer. He was the only black professional player in England during his time with Plymouth Argyle and was expected to become England's first black player, however, he was denied the opportunity when selectors became aware of his heritage.

Modern day footballers

Marcus Rashford MBE – professional footballer who plays for the England national team and premier league club Manchester United. In 2020, Marcus successfully campaigned to combat child hunger by petitioning the UK government to provide economically disadvantaged children with free school meals during school holidays, not just during term time. He was awarded an MBE as acknowledgement of his contribution and efforts.

Raheem Sterling, Jordan Sancho and Ian Wright are all well-known, active anti-racism football campaigners.

Ottobah Cugoano

Abolitionist

Born in 1757 near Ajumako, Ghana, Ottobah Cugoano, also known as John Stuart, was an abolitionist, political activist and natural rights philosopher.

Aged 13, Ottobah was sold into slavery and shipped to Grenada where he worked on an island plantation. In 1772, he was bought by an English merchant who baptised him as John

Stuart. He learnt to read and write and was later freed, joining the 'Sons of Africa' abolition group.

In 1787, he published *Thoughts and Sentiments on the Evil and Wicked Traffic of the Slavery and Commerce of the Human Species*. Despite being one of the first pieces of writing by a black Briton about slavery, the book consists mostly of religious and philosophical argument rather than Cugoano's own experiences.

Cugoano travelled around Britain promoting his book, contributing his voice and first-hand personal testimony to the campaign against the slave trade.

Did you know?

West Indian soldiers and black Britons served in the army and navy during the First World War. The contributions of the 15,204 men who served in the British West Indies Regiment have largely been forgotten in the UK's remembrance of the Great War.

Walter Tull

Professional footballer and soldier

Walter Tull played for Tottenham Hotspur football club. He was one of the first black professional football players in England, later playing for Northampton Town while overcoming racial discrimination. He also become one of the most celebrated black British soldiers of the war, leading men into battle during the

First World War at a time when the army opposed a person of non-European descent becoming an officer.

Walter died aged 29 while leading an attack during the second Battle of the Somme. Private Thomas Billingham, a fellow footballer, saw him killed and tried to retrieve his body so he could have a proper burial. However, Tull's body was never recovered.

Tull is remembered on the memorial wall in the Faubourg d'Amiens cemetery in Arras, along with 35,000 soldiers whose bodies were never recovered from the battlefields, although research by Andy Robertshaw, a military historian, suggests that Tull may have been buried in the unmarked graves at Heninel-Croisilles Road cemetery in northern France. A statue commemorating Walter Tull resides in Northampton.

Ena Collymore

Ena Collymore is Britain's oldest surviving female WWII veteran. She was one of the first women to set sail from the Caribbean to help the allied forces in response to a recruitment advert. She arrived in London having survived a torpedo strike on the boat she travelled on, facing racism and sexism while in the UK. Ena became the first black woman radar operator defending the UK's coast after refusing a clerical job at the War Office.

The Windrush Generation

After the Second World War, the UK invited those from colonies to come to England to help rebuild the country. Due to a shortage of workers, thousands of men and women came to Britain from the Caribbean to work in sectors including manufacturing, public transport and the NHS.

In June 1948, the Empire Windrush arrived at Tilbury Docks, Essex, carrying hundreds of people from the Caribbean on the promise of citizenship and right of abode in the UK as members of the British Empire when they arrived. They were not welcomed with open arms, and neither was citizenship granted. The people lived in cramped conditions and endured racist and unkind remarks. These people became known as the Windrush generation.

Some of the black people you see in England today were born here, and their parents and grandparents are from the Windrush generation. In 2018, people from this generation were wrongly detained, denied legal rights, threatened with deportation, and, in at least 83 cases, wrongly deported from the UK by the Home Office.

The Windrush generation were pivotal in helping us to rebuild our country after World War II, so we must always be grateful to them and celebrate them in British black history.

Cheddar Man

The First Modern Briton

The first modern Briton, thought to have lived around 300 generations ago, had black skin, blue eyes and dark, curly hair. Known as Cheddar Man, Britain's oldest complete skeleton was unearthed more than a century ago in Gough's Cave, Somerset.

DNA analysis revealed that Cheddar Man likely died in his twenties and had a relatively good diet. He lived in Britain when it was almost completely depopulated. Previous populations were wiped out before him – Cheddar Man marked the start of continuous habitation on the island.

Genetically, Cheddar Man belonged to a group of people known as the 'western hunter-gatherers'. His ancestors migrated to Europe from the Middle East after the Ice Age. Today, it is thought that 10 per cent of white British people are descended from this group.

You can read more about Cheddar Man here:

www.newscientist.com/article/2160467-early-briton-from-10000-years-ago-had-dark-skin-and-blue-eyes/.

Eric Irons OBE

The First Black Magistrate

In 1962, Eric Irons OBE became the first black magistrate in the UK, where he sat on the Nottingham bench for 29 years before retiring in 1991.

During the 1950s, Eric campaigned for better employment opportunities, health and education for black workers. As a result of his campaign, black employment increased. Eric was subsequently awarded an OBE in 1977.

What is a magistrate?

Anyone can be a magistrate. They are Justices of the Peace and volunteer judges who sit on criminal and family cases. They are not paid but can claim expenses.

Magistrates can send people to prison for up to six months and they can take people's children away from them.

It's important to have diverse people making decisions about people's lives. These need to be all ages, all backgrounds, and all races, genders, sexuality and communities. I encourage everyone to apply to be a magistrate and qualified lawyers to become magistrates to increase the diversity of the benches from one particular group and age range.

Sir Arthur Lewis

The First Black Professor

Sir William Arthur Lewis (23 January 1915 – 15 June 1991) was a Saint Lucian economist and the James Madison Professor of Political Economy at Princeton University. He was well known for his contributions in the field of economic development and was awarded the Nobel Memorial Prize in Economic Sciences in 1979.

Paul Leroy Robeson

Actor

Paul Robeson (9 April 1898 – 23 January 1976) was an American bass baritone concert artist and stage and film actor. He became famous for his cultural accomplishments and for his political activism.

Paul's political activities began with his involvement with unemployed workers and anti-imperialist students whom he met in Britain. In the United States he became active in the Civil Rights Movement and other social justice campaigns.

Paul Robeson performed in many stage shows in Britain, settling in London for several years with his wife Eslanda. During this period, Robeson became increasingly attuned to the sufferings of people of other cultures, notably the British working class and the colonised people of the British Empire.

Some Role Models from Outside the UK

The following people aren't British, however, they have inspired so many British people from afar.

Nelson Mandela (18 July 1918 – 5 December 2013)

Born in 1918, Nelson Mandela was a South African lawyer, anti-apartheid revolutionary, political leader and philanthropist who served as President of South Africa from 1994 to 1999. He was the country's first black head of state and the first elected in a fully representative democratic election.

Nelson Mandela's political work made him a target for the apartheid regime. When the African National Congress was banned in 1960, he became the leader of Umkhonto we Sizwe (MK), the armed wing of the Congress. In 1962 he was sentenced to five years in prison for instigating a strike and leaving the country illegally. In 1963, Nelson joined other MK leaders in the Rivonia Trial, at the end of which he was sentenced to life in prison for sabotage and attempting to overthrow the South African government. He was finally released from prison in 1990 after over 27 years of unbroken incarceration.

Rosa Parks (4 February 1913 – 24 October 2005)

Rosa Parks was an American activist in the civil rights movement. Racial segregation was normal, with buses having separate white-only and 'coloured' sections. However, Rosa Parks changed that. On December 1, 1955, in Montgomery, Alabama, Rosa refused to give up her seat to a white passenger in the 'coloured' section after the whites-only section was filled.

Rosa's standing in the community and her willingness to become a controversial figure inspired the black community to boycott the Montgomery buses for over a year. This was the first major campaign of the post-war civil rights movement. In November 1956, the courts decided that bus segregation was unconstitutional under the Equal Protection Clause of the 14th Amendment to the US Constitution.

Rosa became an international icon of resistance to racial segregation, organising and collaborating with civil rights leaders including Martin Luther King Jr. Although widely honoured in later years for her act of defiance, Rosa also suffered. She was fired from her job, and received death threats many years afterwards.

In her final years, Rosa suffered from dementia. She received a number of medals, including the Presidential Medal of Freedom, and a posthumous statue in the United States Capitol's National Statuary Hall. After her death in 2005, Rosa was the first woman to lie in the Capitol Rotunda, becoming the thirty-first person to receive this honour.

Rosa Parks Day is commemorated on February 4th, her birthday, in California and Missouri while Ohio and Oregon commemorate the occasion on December 1st, the anniversary of the day she was arrested.

Martin Luther King (15 January 1929 – 4 April 1968)

Martin Luther King Jr. was an American Christian minister and activist. He became the most visible spokesperson and leader in the civil rights movement from 1955 until his assassination in 1968. Inspired by his Christian beliefs and the nonviolent activism of Mahatma Gandhi, King advanced civil rights through non-violence and civil disobedience.

King led the 1955 Montgomery bus boycott and later became the first president of the Southern Christian Leadership Conference (SCLC), leading struggles against segregation and helping to organise non-violent protests. In 1963, King delivered his famous *I Have a Dream* speech on the steps of the Lincoln Memorial.

On October 14, 1964, King won the Nobel Peace Prize for combating racial inequality through non-violent resistance. In his final years, he expanded his focus towards poverty, capitalism, and the Vietnam War.

King was assassinated on April 4th in Memphis, Tennessee, triggering riots in many US cities. He was posthumously awarded the Presidential Medal of Freedom and the Congressional Gold Medal.

Martin Luther King Jr. Day was established as a holiday in cities and states throughout the United States beginning in 1971. Hundreds of streets in the USA have been renamed in his honour.

Did you know?

A fact from my son's teacher, Mr Berry...

Professor Xavier and Magneto in the Marvel comic's X-Men series are inspired by Dr Luther King, Malcolm X and the black civil rights movement. Professor Xavier is in a wheelchair and has the power to enter and control people's minds. He does so for good and for peace.

Magneto was a child in Auschwitz during the Second World War. His mother and father were killed by the Germans. He carries a lot of rage and anger and considers that all humans are bad and cannot change.

Josephine Baker (3 June 1906 – 12 April 1975)

Josephine Baker was an American-born French entertainer, French Resistance agent, and civil rights activist. She was the first black woman to star in a major motion picture, the 1927 silent film *Siren of the Tropics*.

Josephine refused to perform for segregated audiences in the United States and is noted for her contributions to the civil rights movement. She was celebrated by artists of the era, who dubbed her the 'Black Venus', the 'Black Pearl', the 'Bronze Venus', and the 'Creole Goddess'. She aided the French Resistance during World War II.

Josephine was awarded the Croix de Guerre by the French military and was named a Chevalier of the Légion d'honneur by General Charles de Gaulle.

Harriet Tubman (1822 – 1913)

Born Araminta Ross, Harriet Tubman was an abolitionist and political activist. Born into slavery, Harriet escaped and made 13 missions to rescue roughly 70 enslaved people, including friends and family. Her missions were aided by the Underground Railroad – a network of anti-slavery activists and safe houses.

CHALLENGES THAT REMAIN TODAY

It is great to celebrate and understand that black history is part of British history. But today in 2021, problems and challenges remain for black people in Britain.

Much work has been done in the law and by others to tackle inequalities that still exist for black people and minorities in the workplace. Seeking to establish equality and equity, because even in 2021 problems remain facing black and brown people in Britain today. They include:

- Racism
- More black people in prison
- Living in some poor areas
- Lack of job promotion in senior jobs and companies
- Not many people are black or brown in jobs like mine, such as judges
- There are no black or brown people in the Supreme Court
- Being stopped and searched more by the police
- Dying more from Covid-19

In this chapter I explore some of these challenges and issues.

***

In April 2020 following the death of George Floyd in America, some protests started all around the world, despite Covid-19 pandemic restrictions. Black people and white people protested everywhere. The words 'I cannot breathe', in reference to George Floyd's final words, became a metaphor for racism.

Every now and then, Britain is confronted by racism. People talk about it endlessly and carelessly, unsure of what to say, wondering whether they are doing it right. Everyone has an opinion but only a few have any experience. The interest never goes away, but it wanes.

The trouble is not everyone gets to move on. Black people, and other minorities, do not have the luxury of a passing interest in racism. It is their lived reality.

A YouGov poll of black, Asian and minority ethnic Britons surveyed in 2020 revealed the extent to which prejudice and discrimination is embedded in society. Results revealed that two-thirds of black Britons have had a racial slur directly used against them. Three-quarters have been asked where they're "really from".

For many (more than half of respondents), career development has been affected because of their race, with assumptions made about their skills based on their race and a large number reporting racial abuse in the workplace. 70 per cent of respondents believe that the Metropolitan police is institutionally racist. Perhaps unsurprising that two-thirds of black people polled think that racism is still very much in existence. Racism runs deep. It's a systemic problem, requiring a systemic solution.

All Black Lives UK has called for the scrapping of section 60 (which gives the police the right to stop and search), and the abolition of the Met police's gangs' matrix (an intelligence tool that targets suspected gang members). But it doesn't stop there. Health disparities, particularly relating to black women and mental health, racial disparities in the criminal justice system, school exclusions, and race in the workplace are all being called to be addressed.

Racial-sensitivity training must be followed up by continuous change and investment that seeks to genuinely tackle inequalities in everything from housing and education to recruitment, retention and promotion. It means challenging power and redistributing resources.

"When people call for diversity and link it to justice and equality, that's fine. But there's a model of diversity as the difference that makes no difference, the change that brings about no change." ~ Angela Davis.

There are many challenges remaining for black and minority lawyers in the NHS, in income, stop and search, and many more. Challenges remain, for example, like the fact that Covid-19 seems to be killing more black and minority people. But other challenges include progression in the NHS and other areas. Here are examples of some of these:

Black and minority ethnic women are the lowest-earning barristers, reports show.

White male counsel earn the most across professions in England and Wales.

Female barristers from minority ethnic backgrounds are the lowest paid while white male counsel receive the highest incomes, as is shown in figures published by the Bar Standards Board.

That disparity in earnings holds true across the profession when looking at those with similar levels of seniority or working in the same parts of England and Wales or practising in similar areas of the law.

In terms of gender, at the self-employed bar more women than men received fees of up to £150,000 a year, but over that income, the numbers switch. About 9.5% of self-employed female barristers earn £240,000 or more, compared with 26.8% of male barristers.

Wide differences by ethnicity alone were also discovered. Among BAME barristers, there was a far higher proportion (56%) declaring incomes of less than £90,000 a year than among their white colleagues (37%). A few female and minority ethnic barristers did record gross fee incomes of more than £1m.

The board report notes: *"There are also differences in the income of BAME barristers once ethnicity is looked at in more detail, with Black and Black British barristers earning less than Asian and Asian British barristers overall. Black African and Asian Bangladeshi are particularly low earning groups."*

Barrister Alexandra Wilson, founder of Black Women in Law and who was stopped and mistaken for a defendant three times in a day at court, tweeted: *"Ethnic minority female barristers are being paid the least ..."*

In response to the BSB (Bar Standards Board) report, Alexandra recommended that ethnic minority women, in particular, get a fair share of the unallocated junior briefs that are coming into chambers, as well as ensuring that marketing and events are inclusive of and accessible to women.

Challenges Remain in the Judiciary

In *Talking Law* Volume I, I talked about the challenges with diversity, challenges with QC appointments and challenges in the judiciary. Things are improving so we must not lose sight of that. The Judicial appointments have been working very hard on this issue.

The *Diversity of the judiciary: 2020 statistics* report was issued by the government on 17th September 2020. The report is printed below and can also be found at the following link:

https://www.gov.uk/government/statistics/diversity-of-the-judiciary-2020-statistics

More work needs to be done to make judiciary diverse

According to a new report published recently by the Ministry of Justice, an improvement of just one per cent in the past 12 months can be seen in the numbers of women judges.

In the courts in particular just 32% of judges are women and only 26% in more senior court roles.

"Women tended to have a better relative success rate for tribunal applications, compared with the courts," observed Simon Davis.

"In tribunals, women accounted for half of the most senior roles: presidents, chamber presidents, deputy and vice presidents."

When it came to ethnicity, there is again a small improvement: 8% of court judges and 12% of tribunal judges identified as BAME as of 1 April 2020. In 2019, it was 7% of court judges and 11% of tribunal judges.

In senior roles, however, the proportion remains low among people self-identifying as BAME - 4% for the High Court and above.

The number of solicitors in court roles has fallen, with only 32% of court judges coming from non-barrister backgrounds, compared with 63% of tribunal judges.

Simon Davis added: "Across all the legal selection exercises run by the Judicial Appointments Commission (JAC) women made up 50% of applicants, BAME people accounted for 25% and solicitors for 58%. So the good news is that the pool of applicants is increasingly diverse.

"It is however particularly disappointing then to see the present disparity of successful outcomes.

"We will work with colleagues from the Judicial Diversity Forum (JDF) to understand better the reasons for those disparities and to help make sure that application processes are open and fair, while continuing to provide targeted support for solicitors aspiring to judicial office.

"Meanwhile, we also will continue to work with the SRA and LSB, as well as our membership, on increasing the diversity and inclusivity of the profession at all levels."

The NHS

"Doctors from black, Asian and minority ethnic backgrounds have been hindered in their search for senior roles because of widespread 'racial discrimination' in the NHS", according to a report from the Royal College of Physicians.

The RCP, which represents 30,000 of the UK's hospital doctors, found that ingrained 'bias' in the NHS made it much harder for BAME doctors to become a consultant compared with their white counterparts.

"It is clear from the results of this survey that racial discrimination is still a major issue within the NHS," said Dr Andrew Goddard, the RCP's president. "It's a travesty that any healthcare appointment would be based on anything other than ability."

Minority ethnic hospital doctors suffered a double disadvantage in their quest to progress their medical careers by being promoted from a trainee doctor to a consultant, it said.

White doctors applied for fewer posts but were more likely to be shortlisted and offered a job, the RCP found. BAME doctors had less chance of being shortlisted for an interview for a consultant post after their first application, and they were also much less likely to be offered a post after an interview.

The report, which is based on a survey of 399 newly qualified consultants in 2019, said: "White respondents had a 98% chance of being shortlisted after their first application, compared with 91% of black, Asian and minority ethnic respondents.

"The big difference was in likelihood of being offered a post for the first time round: 29% of white respondents were offered a post after being shortlisted for the first time compared with just 12% of BAME respondents."

The RCP examined eight years of data on the experience of doctors, typically in their 30s, who had recently gained their certificate of completion of training, which means they can then apply for their first post as a consultant in a hospital.

Its analysis uncovered "consistent evidence of trainees from BAME backgrounds being less successful at consultant interview. This is despite adjustment for potential confounding factors. The results ... suggest there is bias that needs to be acted on."

Roger Kline, a research fellow at Middlesex University and an expert in racial discrimination in the NHS, said the findings proved BAME medics suffered from "systemic discrimination".

"These findings are appalling and confirm what many doctors across all medical specialities have long suspected has been occurring.

"These patterns of discrimination are really hard for individual doctors to challenge so the medical profession as a whole, and their employers, need to finally accept systemic discrimination exists and take decisive action."

NHS blood unit systemically racist, internal report finds.

The RCP found that BAME doctors have more chance of being shortlisted after their first application than they did when it first sounded the alarm about inequity in career progression in 2018. That prompted NHS England to include those findings in its medical workforce race equality standard, which is meant to eradicate bias on racial grounds.

Research in 2018 found that black doctors in the NHS in England are paid almost £10,000 a year less than white colleagues, while the gap for black nurses is £2,700.

Charlie Massey, the chief executive of the General Medical Council, which regulates the profession, said: "All doctors should have the same opportunities to fulfil their potential and it is unacceptable if there are biases that prevent this from happening."

Joan Saddler, the director of partnerships and equality at the NHS Confederation, which represents health service bosses, said: "Leaders are clear that there should be no room for discrimination of any kind within the NHS... The NHS is making some progress on this issue but, clearly, there is much further to go."

The NHS in England has set itself a target of ensuring that by 2025 at least 19% of those at every pay level are of BAME origin. Overall BAME people make up 17.5% of its staff.

A spokesperson for the NHS in England said: "It is unacceptable for anyone to be treated unfairly because of their race or any other protected characteristic.

"The NHS belongs to us all, and as part of the People Plan, NHS employers are committed to increasing black, Asian and minority ethnic representation across their leadership teams as well as eliminating discrimination and inequality."

Challenges in Other Sectors

Challenges in Education and Academics

Whilst we celebrate diversity in law and black excellence as well as allies, many challenges remain.

Women and black academics remain under-represented at professor level with only 1% of UK university professors being black (Higher Education Statistics Agency).

According to Dr Begum, around a "quarter of British postgraduates are from ethnic minorities, there is clearly no shortage of qualified black and minority academics seeking elevation to senior teaching and research roles in our universities."

Black and minority ethnic staff continue to be under-represented.

Challenges for Career Progression and Further Reading

Some useful reports from 2019 and 2020:

Judicial diversity

https://assets.publishing.service.gov.uk/government/uploads/system/uploads/attachment_data/file/918529/diversity-of-the-judiciary-2020-statistics-web.pdf
https://assets.publishing.service.gov.uk/government/uploads/system/uploads/attachment_data/file/918529/diversity-of-the-judiciary-2020-statistics-web.pdf

Latest Judicial Diversity and Inclusion Strategy

https://www.judiciary.uk/wp-content/uploads/2020/11/Judicial-Diversity-and-Inclusion-Strategy-2020-2025.pdf

QC

If you haven't already seen this, you may find it helpful – the appointment of QCs and from what groups:

https://lnprodstorage.z35.web.core.windows.net/Counsel/2021/QC%20Announcements/lvJ2sVn7d/html/index.html

BEING AN ALLY AND BEING ACTIVELY ANTI-RACIST

How to Make a Difference
How to be an Ally

It was notable on all the Black Lives Matter protests, that the people marching were not just the black and brown people but allies. These were allies from all backgrounds. White people, young people, friends, neighbours, colleagues and strangers. Together they were protesting. This gave me hope. I am very much about educating and learning and finding out how we can all help, whatever our characteristics.

We all have a voice, and we can all use it, whether in protesting or petitions or using other platforms.

This video by John Amaechi OBE for BBC Bitesize is very helpful.
It's two minutes long yet very powerful.
Not being a racist is not enough.
We can do something.
We need to be anti-racist, anti-Semitic, anti-homophobic and so on. But we need to do this actively and not passively.

This is what John said in the video, and what he said is a good place to plan to be an ally.

John Amaechi is a psychologist, a New York Times best-selling author and a former NBA basketball player. He is from Manchester. He was the first openly gay black NBA player. In the wake of the George Floyd killing and the Black Lives Matter protests, and at a time when many people want to learn how they can be better allies for black people, John was asked what it means to be anti-racist.

"There's a big difference between being not-racist and being anti-racist. I know it doesn't seem like it. I know that both of these things seem equally good, but they're not."

Video Transcript

John: *There's a big difference between being not-racist and being anti-racist. I know it doesn't seem like it. I know that both of these things seem equally good, but they're not.*

Think of an interaction. I'm afraid you've probably had one right? With somebody, maybe even somebody you respect, maybe even someone you love, who says something that's racist, does something that's racist, behaves in a way that's racist. Someone who's not-racist: they won't say or do anything in that moment. They want to not rock the boat. They don't want to be upstanding. Instead, not-racists: they tend to be bystanders. But afterwards, after the event, they'll find other people who are also not-racist and they'll talk to each other about, well, that was terrible, that thing that happened the other day. I would never say anything like that. Anti-racists are different and they come in all shapes and sizes. They come in all ages.

Anti-racists are constantly looking around to say, what tools do I have available to make it clear that this is not acceptable? And this, this is what anti-racists do.

It's not that they stand up at the dinner table when their uncle's a little bit racist and kick the turkey off. That's not it.

But what they do is they say, "I'm sorry uncle John. That's not acceptable. That's racist." Quietly and respectfully.

What they do is they make sure that they never miss an opportunity to let the world know where they stand, even if they can't change everything. You're probably in a position where other people have a lot more power around you. I know how that feels. Sometimes, we sit and we look around us and we think, how can I possibly change all this? And sometimes you can't. But what you can do is make sure wherever you go, people know where you stand. They know that you're an anti-racist. You become a beacon of light that way. You become someone who makes other people want to be anti-racist too. You've got tools at your disposal. Learn. Read. And make everybody clear where you stand.

I hope this helps. It is the best example I can find, and I suggest that it explains how to be anti-racist. How to be an ally. Sometimes, it's hard to stand up and be counted. But if black lawyers, for example, can still be mistaken for defendants in their place of work (magistrates court) as can Alexandra Wilson the barrister and author, then we still have a long way to go.

Things are changing, and just as young people demand change. I believe change is coming.

BEING POSITIVE

A note on positivity. We all need to be positive. What can your organisation do, or companies do, or people's businesses and companies do to still be positive on the issue of diversity and also Black Lives Matter? Can you take positive action?

Positive action vs POSITIVE discrimination

What is the difference between these?

Positive Discrimination is illegal here in the UK. Creating a job specifically for a protected characteristic – be that gender, ability, orientation, age or race/ethnicity – is illegal under the Equality Act 2010. It also annoys people.

Positive Action is legal. This is where companies create cultures and talent development programmes to ensure talented and qualified people from underrepresented groups get an opportunity to thrive. From entry-level to leadership. From supply chain to sponsorship. Moving beyond meritocracy to intentional opportunities for talent through a well-thought-out narrative.

Sure, there are people who don't get it and think it's just about hard work but for those who are happy to go on a journey of listening and learning it is a good starter to be building the inclusive cultures many organisations think they already have, but don't.

This is what positive action looks like. All companies can do this. Or try to do this.

Conclusion

I am not a historian. I am a lawyer and I love history. I enjoy going to museums and galleries and often wonder where all the black and brown people are. What is their contribution to black history? I don't want to travel all the way to Liverpool to find out about slavery, or to Bristol or Falmouth in Cornwall. I would like to be able to read about it as part of everyday life which is what inspired me to write this book. Britain is a small island with an incredibly rich and diverse history. Let this unite us not divide us. Because all black history is all our history.

I did not include the sports stars and the TV stars and the obvious celebrities that older readers may be familiar with. For example, Trevor McDonald and Moira Stewart whom I grew up with, reading the news on TV or Joan Armatrading whose music I love. Instead, I deliberately chose lesser-known characters who played a forgotten yet pivotal role in our history.

I hope you found this book as interesting as I did in writing about some of these brilliant figures from history. Of course, it is not all the history, just a brief yet significant snapshot in time. But I hope that, going forward, we can all celebrate black history together, and that you continue your exploration into our lesser-known past. It is my hope that Black History Month will soon become part of our everyday history and that a more true and accurate reflection of history will be taught as part of the curriculum.

If you are a teacher, please use this book as a learning resource. I have also included a list of recommended books to aid your learning in your school and in your workplace.

I am grateful to my children for encouraging me to write this book. I am also grateful to the brilliant teachers at my children's school who said there was an appetite for the book. I am especially grateful for the leadership of Mr How the headteacher who understood the importance of diversity and community. Thank you to Miss Hardy, Silva, Miss Noden, Miss Ulett and all of the team who recognise the importance of black history. And thank you to Mr Dan Berry for reminding me of the X-Men and Marvel comics.

I hope that you will send me some of the hidden figures from black British history that you have discovered for me to write about in future editions of this book.

Activities

You can do some of these activities during Black History Month with children at school or at home:

Choose one figure from history and find out more information about them.

Can you make a PowerPoint presentation of one of the characters from the book?

Can you find a famous figure NOT in this book?

What is your heritage? Might you be related to the 'Beachy Head Woman', for example?

Can you think of some books you could write and an era in history you could find out about?

What type of food do they eat in the Caribbean where the Windrush generation came from?

What type of food did they eat in the world wars? Can you find out?

What clues does archaeology give us about history and black history?

What area of history would you like to learn about next?

If you could build a time machine, what part of history would you like to go back to and why?

Share your answers and activities with @sallypenni1 using the hashtag #blackhistoryisallourhistory.

Further Reading

Little Leaders: Bold Women in Black History by Vashti Harrison

Young, Gifted and Black by Jamia Wilson

Black and British: A Forgotten History by David Olusoga

Black and British: A Short, Essential History (for young readers) by David Olusoga

100 Great Black Britons by Patrick Vernon and Angelina Osbourne

Charities

Half of the proceeds from sales of this book will help these charities:

The Black Curriculum – set up and run by CEO Lavinya Stennett.

ACLT – a charity that helps children find bone marrow donors from black and minority communities.

OTHER BOOKS BY SALLY SJ PENNI

Found at www.sallypenniauthor.co.uk

Legal books:
Talking Law 1
Talking Law 2
Talking Law 3
Talking Law and Skills - Skills for Lawyers of the Future and Future Lawyers - published April 2021

Books on Law:
Penni on Data Protection - coming soon
Penni on Basic Employment Rights and post-Covid litigation

Professional development and career development books:
Penni on Purpose - A sense of purpose
Penni on Confidence - Triple C - How to have more confidence, clarity and connection and beat your imposter syndrome
Penni on Skills

Children's books:
Rosie and the Unicorn series of books

Twitter: @rosieandthe
Instagram: @rosieandtheunicorn
Facebook: @rosieandtheunicorn
Rosie and the Unicorn
Rosie and the Unicorn Activity Book

Coming Soon:
Rosie and the Unicorn go on Holiday - out December 2021
Rosie and the Unicorn go to Court - out March 2022

Novels:

Sally Penni writes fictional novels under a pen name. This genre is crime thriller and psychological thriller.

Book tours:
Sally does book tours, book readings and speaks in school assemblies to children of all ages about her career as a barrister and mum, as a way to encourage more young people to enter law.

Contact:
www.sallypenniauthor.co.uk
Sally is available for Literature Festivals
Book readings
School assemblies speaking on law, gender, career, early law makers and more.
Follow her:
Twitter: @sallypenni1
Instagram: @sjsallypenni